COMMITTED
TO CHRISTIANITY

A P E N T E C O S T A L
C O M M U N I T Y

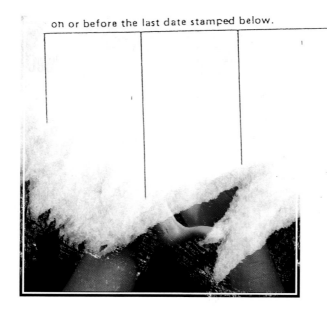

S Y L V I A   A N D   B A R R Y
S U T C L I F F E

RMEP

RELIGIOUS AND MORAL EDUCATION PRESS

Religious and Moral Education Press
An imprint of Chansitor Publications Ltd,
a wholly owned subsidary of Hymns Ancient & Modern Ltd
St Mary's Works, St Mary's Plain
Norwich, Norfolk NR3 3BH

First published 1994

ISBN 1-85175-021-5

Acknowledgements
The Authors and Publisher would like to thank the leaders and
brethren of the New Testament Assembly, Tooting, particularly
those whose interviews appear in this book, for their generous
help. We are especially indebted to Dahlia Cowan for her time
and care as our principal contact during all stages of work.

We are also grateful to J. Wippell & Co. Ltd, Exeter, for the loan
of several items used in photography.

Designed and typeset by Topics Visual Information, Exeter

Photography by Michael Burton-Pye

Printed in Singapore by Tien Wah Press for
Chansitor Publications Ltd, Norwich

CONTENTS

INTRODUCTION

The books in this **Faith and Commitment** series give you the chance to look at religions and religious denominations (groups within religions) through the personal reflections of people with a religious commitment.

To create these books, we visited local religious communities in different parts of Britain. We talked to people across the range of ages and roles you'd expect to find in a community – parent, child, grandparent, priest, community worker. That is, we interviewed people like you and your family, your friends, the people where you live. We asked them all the same questions and we've used the themes of those questions as chapter headings in the books.

Each chapter contains extracts from those interviews. People interpret our questions as they want to. They talk freely in their own words about religious ideas and personal experiences, putting emphasis where they think it belongs for them. The result is a set of very individual insights into what religion means to some of the people who practise it. A lot of the insights are spiritual ones, so you may have had similar thoughts and experiences yourself, whether or not you consider yourself a 'religious' person.

You will see that some pages include FACT-FINDER boxes. These are linked to what people say in the interview extracts on these pages. They give you bits of back-up information, such as a definition or where to look up a reference to a prayer or a piece of scripture. Remember that these books are not textbooks. We expect you to do some research of your own when you need to. There are plenty of sources to go to and your teacher will be able to help.

There are also photographs all through the books. Some of the items you can see belong to the people whose interview extracts appear on those pages. Most of these items have personal significance. Some have religious significance, too. They are very special to the people who lent them for particular but different reasons, like special things belonging to you.

Committed to Christianity: A Pentecostal Community introduces you to nine Pentecostal Christians from the New Testament Assembly church in Tooting, south-west London. The New Testament Assembly was founded in Jamaica in 1954. It now has more than forty churches worldwide, in Africa, the U.S.A., Canada and Britain, where it is a member of the British Council of Churches.

SYLVIA AND BARRY SUTCLIFFE

ABOUT ME

NAME: *Asa D*

WHAT I DO: *I'm twelve years old. I go to school in Wimbledon.*

MY FAMILY: *I come from a church family, a religious family. We go to church every Sunday. I've got one brother, Darren. My mum fosters. My foster-brother's name's Victor. My mum fosters quite a few children.*

SOME OF MY SPECIAL INTERESTS: *I like drawing – artistic drawings – and designing. I'd like to be a graphic designer. I like playing basketball and sometimes football, and I play badminton.*

NAME:	*Judith D*
WHAT I DO:	*I was a nurse for twenty years. Now I work as a probation officer.*
MY FAMILY:	*I foster. I love children so much. I've got two sons of my own and I've fostered five children already. The present one is my sixth.*
MY ROLE IN THE RELIGIOUS COMMUNITY:	*I'm assistant catering officer for the church. There's another sister who's in charge. But I seem to do so much work here, because we do have a lot of major functions. I don't mind. I thoroughly enjoy it. My colleague and I complement each other so well. I'm not a cook. She does the cooking. I do the sharing out, preparing, that sort of thing.*

MORE ABOUT ME

I came to the conclusion many years ago now that I love people. No matter who you are, I can always find something nice to say about you. I'll make sure I search for something nice about you.

I've worked in two caring professions. I care about people. I could never live alone. Some people are very selfish. I couldn't be, because I believe this world is not for me alone.

I work full time and I've got three children, so it is a bit difficult sometimes finding time for everything. But I organize my work. I take the children with me, and they do like to be here in the church.

FACT-FINDER

Sister
Another (female) member of the church, not Judith's actual sister. Christians sometimes call each other 'brother' or 'sister' because they think of themselves as all belonging to the 'family' of Christians. God is like a father to them all.

NAME:	*Martin W*

WHAT I DO: *I'm at school. Year 10.*

MY FAMILY: *There's my mum and dad and my two sisters.*

SOME OF MY SPECIAL INTERESTS: *I'm interested in computers. I want to go into computer programming. I enjoy being out with my friends and sometimes I enjoy school work — it depends on what lesson. I like drama, French, maths and science. I'm not too keen on geography. I'm studying for GCSEs at the moment.*

NAME:	*Verona W*

MY FAMILY: *I'm married. I've got three children — two girls and a boy.*

MORE ABOUT ME

I was brought up in a Christian home. My parents, grandparents and so forth were Christian.

I view God basically as my father, my friend. He's a fatherly figure that I can look up to, that I can say 'Dad' to. You know, with your natural father you say 'Dad'. I just think I'm a daughter of God. He won't let anything happen to me. With your own children, you want the best for them. I know that God wants the best for me.

NAME:	*Yvonne*

MY FAMILY: *I came from Guyana in South America to England at the age of twenty-five. I'm now sixty-one-and-a-half years old. I'm the mother of seven children and have thirteen grandchildren.*

MY ROLE IN THE RELIGIOUS COMMUNITY: *I come from a history of singers and actors, so I'm able to minister for the Lord in song. At the Over-50s Club, we've just brought a choir together. I've kindly been asked to conduct and lead it. We help those that are housebound.*

WHAT I DO

I always say to the Lord, 'Help me to help others.' Because that's why we're saved. We're not saved for a good jump about and a nice morning service – clap your hands, say 'Hallelujah', then go home until next Sunday. No, no. We're saved to serve.

For instance, I work with the Metropolitan Police. I'm an Appropriate Adult. When young people are arrested, the Police call me at all hours of the night. I go out to counsel the young people. I pray for them. I see that they're getting all their legal rights. I don't get paid.

It's the love of Jesus that let's me do what I do. It's the Christ in me that keeps me bubbling, keeps me singing, keeps me loving everybody. It's a beautiful life.

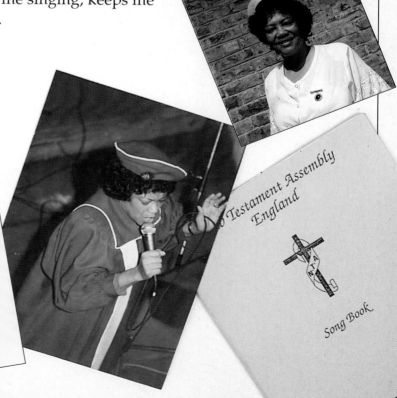

FACT-FINDER

Minister for the Lord in song
Use her singing voice in God's service.

Hallelujah
Hebrew word meaning 'Praise the Lord'. For Pentecostals, 'Hallelujah' is the highest praise that people can give to God.

Saved
Pentecostals believe that all humans sin (do wrong, break God's rules) during their lives. So, before they die, everyone needs to be saved by God from punishment for their sins.

Pentecostals believe that people are saved by God when they confess that there is sin and believe in their hearts that Jesus is the Son of God and that he died to save them from their sins.

NAME: *David*

WHAT I DO: *I started off as an accountant. Now I'm a minister with the New Testament Assembly and a member of its Executive Board.*

MY FAMILY: *I'm married with three children.*

MY ROLE IN THE RELIGIOUS COMMUNITY: *My main role in this church is that I worship here. As a minister, I lead praise and worship sometimes. I preach when I'm asked to. I take the Eucharist – anything I'm called to do. I sit on the steering group that plans the services for the next quarter and I network with other churches, other religions, other communities.*

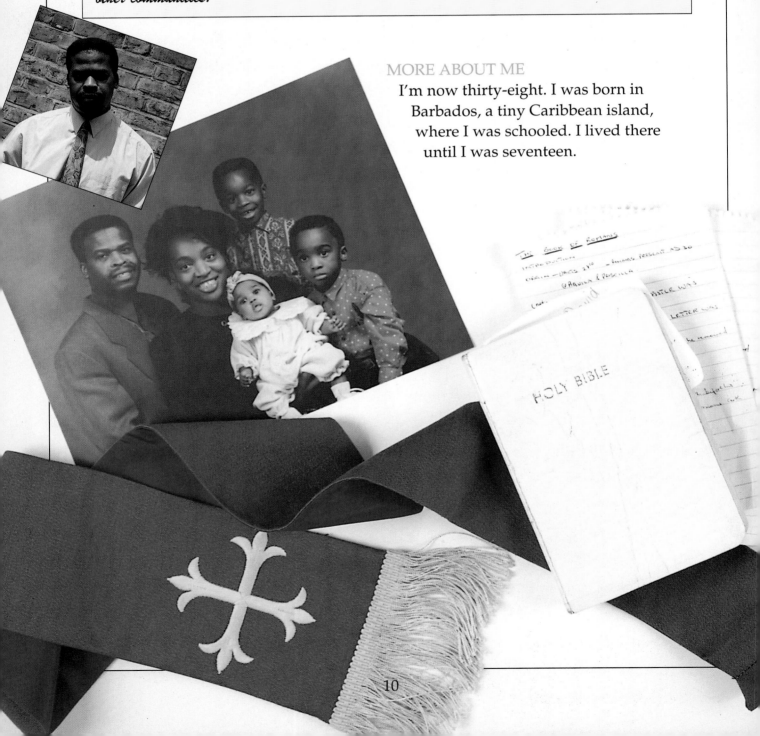

MORE ABOUT ME

I'm now thirty-eight. I was born in Barbados, a tiny Caribbean island, where I was schooled. I lived there until I was seventeen.

HOLY BIBLE

I feel strongly about not drinking or swearing. I don't take drugs. I'm not into that. Mum and Dad allow me to go to parties and people may be smoking. I've got friends that do it, but they don't pressure me.

Another thing is, me and my friends, we all sit in a bunch at church. We'll sit either at the front or the back. Every Sunday without fail somebody'll come up to us after church and tell us to stop talking. But it's literally impossible. Sometimes the preacher can go on and on or just not talk the same language as us.

There was one particular preacher who came from Jamaica, and the way he came over really did touch us. He spoke the way that we speak, like when we're out together. He was referring to music that we listen to outside church. It did get to us. I mean, that's how I think church should be more.

A lot of the older generation don't understand that the reason why we talk is because the preacher doesn't give us a buzz. There's nothing there for us. The preacher preaches to the older generation, to born-again Christians. People say we should go up to the preacher after church, but it's hard. I've got cousins that came here, but they've dropped out.

MARTIN W

FACT-FINDER

Born-again Christians
Many Christians say that becoming a Christian is like being born again, i.e. new Christians are making a completely fresh start in life. Here, by 'born-again Christians' Martin means people who have become fully committed Christians as adults, either for the first time or after a time when they had rejected or drifted away from Christianity.

I know how God has treated us. I know how the Lord has shown us things, brought us through when we've had difficult moments, fought our battles for us. I want that to be passed on to my children. I want them to have that joy.

But you can't force it on them. You can talk with them, pray with them. Then it's up to them. Everyone's got to work life out for themselves. I've started sowing the seeds. Eventually, they'll grow and bloom.

VERONA W

I 've got strong feelings about children – and about abusers of children. I've seen the trauma it causes.

There are some parents who do not care about their children. They just have them and leave them to their own devices. Because of my Christian upbringing, I know that children need to be directed. If my children rebel, I say to them, 'Well, the Bible says this....'

I was brought up in Jamaica by a strict grandmother. There it wasn't just your family who would bring you up. Other people shared in your life, your upbringing, as well. I've brought that attitude here with me and I've taken it into the church. I've said to the brethren of the church, 'If my children do something wrong, they can be disciplined. I will not be annoyed as long as it's within reason.'

I do the same for them, even if they're going to be upset. I can't see a child doing something wrong and not talk to them about it. So it's like your children growing up in a bigger family. People here are very loving.

JUDITH D

FACT-FINDER

Brethren
Literally 'brothers'. Judith means the other members of the church, women as well as men. (See also page 7.)

I feel strongly about child abuse. Abusing children is wrong. And I feel strongly about rape.

ASA D

I know what God can do. I know God can do many things. The things he's done for me, I can hardly believe. It just happens in such a miraculous way. Sometimes I say to my friend, 'I just don't deserve this. God's doing so many things for me.'

But if you just give up your life to God then things happen. If you say, 'Lord, take my life. Have your own way with my life. Don't let me have any more control of it, you take control. Just lead me every day as I go on.' You get up in the morning. You're going out to work. You say, 'Lord, I don't know what I'm going to face today, but just lead the way for me.'

For example, there was my college exam. I hadn't studied. I couldn't study because where I was the environment wasn't right for studying. I went into college that day and I said, 'Lord, I want to prove you now. I don't know anything and I don't know what I'm going to do on the paper.'

When I got the paper, I read all the questions and didn't know the answer to one. I said, 'Lord, I have to pass this exam. I know you're there and I want to prove you. I've proved you lots of times but I want to prove you definitely this time.'

It was a multiple-choice paper. I just closed my eyes and started ticking down the answers. I didn't even read the questions. When I gave in my paper, my friend asked, 'How was it?'

I said, 'Don't ask me. I don't know. I didn't do it myself.' Next day at college I got my paper back – with every answer right. Not even one wrong.

My friend didn't believe in God or anything before that. She couldn't understand how I could say things like God is going to do this or that. But she thought about my experience and started going to church.

DESREEN S

T he Bible says that it's not by might nor power nor wisdom either that things are achieved. It's by God's Spirit. Theology alone can't do what God can do.

We do study the word of God, though. For example, through this church, I've just finished a course in theology at St David's College, Lampeter. I gained a good grade, B, at fifty-nine. On the course we had to write theology. That's fine. But, in the end, 'God is Spirit, and they that worship him must worship him in spirit and in truth'.

We teach the word of God, we preach it. But it's the personal relationship with God that's important. It comes from an inner desire. I don't know how you view Jesus, but I know I wanted him. When you have this desire in your heart, God will lead you.

That's why we dance and shout and praise God in church. Going to church isn't like some people think – flat or boring. It's not. There's a joy you cannot explain.

I was watching a very learned gentleman on television once. He said how he despised Christians when they put their hands in the air as if to say, 'We've got it.' But that's not what we're saying. We're giving praise to God. It's not a game. It's not a myth. It's not a figment of our imaginations. It's not an attitude. It's not hysteria.

Life can be hard. Many of us came here as foreigners, and it wasn't easy climbing that ladder. So when you see what God's done for you, you give praise. You know when you go to a football match and your side scores a goal? What do you do? You're up on your feet. You're cheering.

YVONNE

FACT-FINDER

Theology
The study of God and human beings' relationship with God, using a formal approach based on reasoning and scholars' research.

'God is Spirit ...'
See John 4:24 in the Bible.

Continuity in the churches is important. The Church of England has got itself into a dispute about women priests. Those things tend to divide Christians. I believe that the churches should come together more. We're all worshipping the same God. It seems to me there are too many divisions, too many institutions.

Christianity is all about people. In this day and age we need to move forward. It's time for the churches to come out and show the community they can do things – like helping the homeless, running housing associations, schemes helping people get work. Church members should be doing practical jobs as opposed to just going to church on Sunday. There should be projects in areas of need.

I mean, Jesus went out and did things. He didn't stay in a church preaching, he actually went out. So really we as Christians should be ready to go out and use whatever talents we've got – teaching, engineering – where the real needs are.

RAYMOND S

FACT-FINDER

Church of England • Women priests

The Church of England is the English branch of the world-wide Anglican church. In the Anglican church, only a priest can carry out the ceremony which consecrates (makes sacred) the bread and wine at a Eucharist service.

On 11 November 1992, the members of the General Synod (the 'parliament' of the Church of England) voted by a narrow majority in favour of allowing women to become priests. The subject is still controversial.

MY FAVOURITE FESTIVAL

Easter is a special festival for me. It's so central to the Christian faith. There's a special feeling about Easter. There's a feeling of hope, of birth being given to Christians, because without Easter there wouldn't be a church. With all its celebrations, Easter really gives faith, new life and reality to it.
That's special to me.

I think of the suffering Christ – what he had to go through when he could have chosen not to. I see and recognize that he indeed suffered immensely and that out of that suffering came new life, resurrection. I hold on to that. It tells me that, though it may be dark, at some stage the light will come and everything will be different.

DAVID

FACT-FINDER

Resurrection
Rising (of Jesus) from the dead. This is celebrated every Easter.

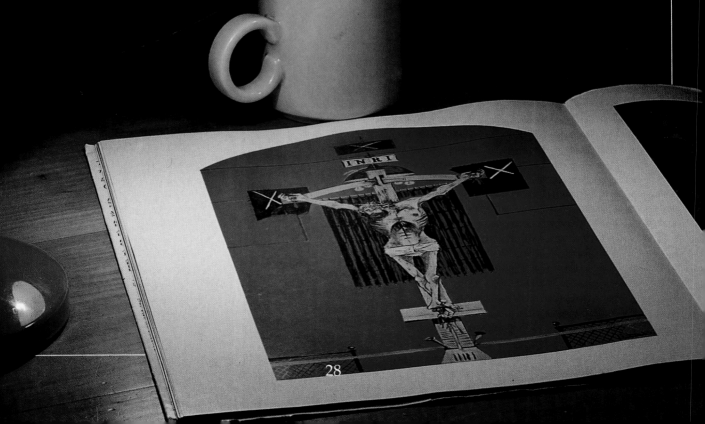

28

I like Harvest Thanksgiving. That's from when I was a young child, bringing in the baskets of fruit.

It's important to give God thanks for the simple things in life – potatoes, carrots – because we're fortunate in this part of the world. We can eat three square meals a day, go to Macdonald's if we want. You see those pictures from places like Africa, children scraping a few rice grains together. So really, Harvest is important. It's saying thank you to God for sustaining us. It's a time of thanksgiving, a time to appreciate what we've been given.

After the service in church, what's been gathered in goes to the old people's homes or the needy.

RAYMOND S

I wouldn't say we have festivals as such. The only time we do some extra celebrations is at Christmas and at Easter. But they're not different from any other times in that we still come together in fellowship to worship.

DAHLIA

I wouldn't say I've got a particular festival that's a favourite. We don't really celebrate festivals as such.

VERONA W

C hristmas is my favourite. It's the presents, the way it comes over.

Two years ago I got a suit and Mum said I could wear it to church on Christmas Day. When I walked in, everyone turned their head. I like coming to church on Christmas Day because you can show off your presents or say what you've got and compare it with each other.

MARTIN W

M y favourite festival's Christmas. I get presents, and it's when Christ was born. We have a Christmas service in the morning. The preaching's about Christmas. Sometimes there are plays at Christmas and Easter.

On the last day of the year, we have a service all through the night and into the next year. In the morning we leave.

We have our National Convention and an International Convention. The International Convention is when all the New Testament churches come to our church. We have delegates from other countries. That's once a year, in August. It's livelier than a normal service. We have groups coming to sing, other choirs and everything.

We've just had our National Convention. That's our convention, and some of the other churches come to support our church. All the other churches do their own conventions as well.

ASA D

30

Our conventions are the big events of the year. Other churches call them convocations. A convention is a gathering of the brethren of the churches. We are the headquarters of an international church, the New Testament Assembly, so we have other branches in Jamaica, in Canada, in the States and lots of other branches in England.

We meet in August, Bank Holiday week, for seven days. That is usually so beautiful. We have different preachers, different things go on. Each church reports on how it's progressing. We also have concerts, musical events. Lots of Pentecostal groups sing gospel songs. There are different soloists – some beautiful soloists – and choirs, and not just from our church. We invite other Pentecostal churches – like the New Testament Church of God, Church of God of Prophecy, Church of God in Christ – and they do join in.

JUDITH D

My favourite festival is Crusade. They call it Convention here. People come together. We get a lot of singing in church. I like that. People come in, accept Christ.

We try to minister to people, win souls. We witness to them, tell them who God is and that he's alive. We tell them that the great thing in our lives has been to accept him. We try to win souls for God. People get saved. That's why I really love Crusade.

DESREEN S

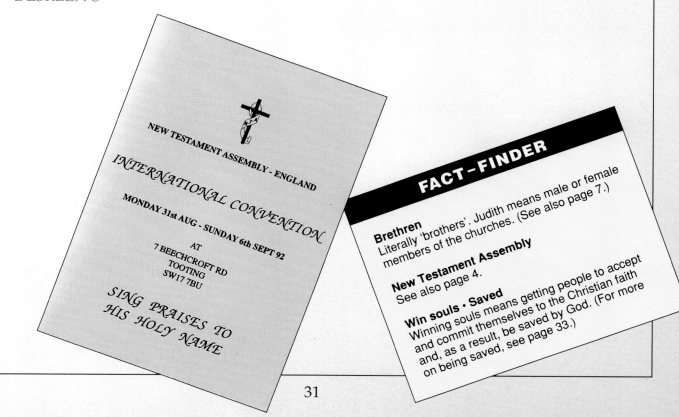

NEW TESTAMENT ASSEMBLY - ENGLAND

INTERNATIONAL CONVENTION

MONDAY 31st AUG - SUNDAY 6th SEPT 92

AT

7 BEECHCROFT RD
TOOTING
SW17 7BU

SING PRAISES TO
HIS HOLY NAME

FACT-FINDER

Brethren
Literally 'brothers'. Judith means male or female members of the churches. (See also page 7.)

New Testament Assembly
See also page 4.

Win souls · Saved
Winning souls means getting people to accept and commit themselves to the Christian faith and, as a result, be saved by God. (For more on being saved, see page 33.)

A
SPECIAL MOMENT

I think the moment of my conversion was the most significant thing that's happened to me.

My parents were Christians, but when I got older I wasn't a Christian. I had quite a good job. I was in the world. I had Christian beliefs and occasionally went to church, but there were a lot of things wrong in my life. One day, I was washing my car and I just stood, searching my soul.

At that time I was sharing a house with a guy who came to this church. He invited me to one of the Young People's Meetings. At first I said, 'Well, no. I'm not really interested.' But then I thought I'd come along.

I met the people and listened to their way of praising the Lord and their message. Being a bit older, I'd seen the worldly side of life. The way they worshipped seemed really genuine. It touched my heart.

About four or five months later, I was in a meeting there. Most people around me had been saved and they were saying, 'Why don't you be saved, then?' I said, 'I'm not really ready now.' So they said,'Think about it. Really, today can be the day.'

I actually fought. I closed my eyes and prayed. I felt I wanted to be a Christian. I wanted to change my life. I felt very strange, very light-headed. I'm normally a very strong-willed person. I don't class myself as being very spiritual. But I felt a change in me. I went outside and the whole street looked very different, and the people. I felt really elated. My spirit felt lifted up high.

I knew I was different then. I remember it as a big change in my life. I'd accepted the Lord into my life. I got baptized about eight months after that.

My baptism was interesting. I had to go down into the water – total immersion. We've got a pool here. You go into the water and receive the baptism of the Holy Ghost. Then you start working for Christ.

Once you're baptized, you think, 'I'm a Christian.' Your life should be a shining example, but it's still hard. You make errors. I remember after I got baptized I was driving my car and someone cut me up. I swore! I shouldn't have done that.

It's in small ways that you realize your life has changed.
Slowly your life adapts. You read your Bible a bit
more, pray a bit more, you're more compassionate.

Your tastes change. I used to watch some fairly
horrific videos. Now I don't. My music taste
has got very conservative. No obscene lyrics.
I'll go to college and friends there will invite
me to parties. Sometimes I'll say, 'I can come
to your party, but I've been there before.
You'll have a few beers, get drunk, try
and chase women. Those things are
temporary pleasures. When you get to
know the Lord, it lasts for eternity, for
ever.'

I try to love my neighbour. I try to
live in a Christian way and cast out
the old me. I tend to be more tolerant,
I think. I'm less aggressive. I look into myself more.

One day we're going to die, right? You have to say to yourself,
'OK, if the Bible is wrong, I've made a mistake. But if the Bible is right...'
What are you going to do? I try to live the best life I can.

RAYMOND S

FACT-FINDER

Conversion
When he fully accepted and committed himself
to the Christian faith.

Saved
Pentecostals believe that all humans sin
(do wrong, break God's rules) during their lives.
So, before they die, everyone needs to be
saved by God from punishment for their sins.

Pentecostals believe that people are saved by
God when they confess that there is sin and
believe in their hearts that Jesus is the Son of
God and that he died to save them from their
sins.

Soul
Innermost self. The part of a person that
Christians believe survives after their body dies.

Baptism of the Holy Ghost
The Holy Ghost is God's Holy Spirit. In the
Pentecostal church, receiving the baptism of
the Holy Spirit is a personal experience not a
church ceremony. It may happen before, after
or at someone's baptism in the pool. The
person feels in very close contact with the Holy
Spirit. (See also Verona's description of her
experience on pages 34–35.)

I suppose I can only speak for myself about what happened. Before my husband and I were saved, God was obviously doing things in our lives without us actually being committed to him. Then my mum had a stroke. It was bad, but she was back up again in three months. I think it all spinned from that. Then the Lord spoke to my husband at home in a dream to say, 'I've called you. Follow me.' So we decided to come to church.

It was a Sunday afternoon. I can remember it was quite strange. It was as if the Lord had said to me, 'Here I am. Accept me.' I got up and said, 'Yes.' I can remember being at the altar. Counsellors came up with us and prayed with us. Then afterwards we went to the prayer room. All four counsellors were crying. We were in tears. We cried for days.

I was never baptized previously. I always wanted not to turn back once I'd committed myself to God. Now I *was* baptized. My husband and I were baptized together. It was a first for our church. We were the first couple ever to have been baptized together in the same pool at the same time.

Receiving the baptism of the Holy Ghost, that was a very exciting thing for me. It was about three months or so after I'd given myself to the Lord. I don't know how to put it into words. You can read in the Bible how in the upper room, on the day of Pentecost, the disciples received the baptism of the Holy Ghost.

I think the majority of Pentecostal Christians do strive to reach the point where you can receive the baptism of the Holy Ghost. It was one of my aims. I really wanted to be at that level with God. I needed the comfort that he'd promised me. Once you've given yourself to the Lord, he is with you all the time. But you get an extra inner help when you do receive the baptism of the Holy Spirit.

It was a marvellous experience. It happened in a prayer meeting. I can remember saying, 'Lord, I need this. I'm not going to give up until you baptize me in the Holy Spirit.' I really travailled – by that, I mean that I really prayed. I was really seeking God's face, really seeking him. Then the Holy Spirit came down and I felt enlightened, like I was floating, just not there.

FACT-FINDER

Saved
Verona means before they accepted and committed themselves to the Christian faith and were therefore saved. (See also page 33.)

Holy Ghost
God's Holy Spirit.

How in the upper room ...
See Acts 2:1–4.

Travailled
Laboured, worked hard and painfully, as a woman does when having a baby.

I praise God that I did receive the Holy Spirit. Now he's there with me all the time. Anything I'm doing, he instructs me, he guides me. It's just a wonderful feeling to know that you have the Lord with you all the time.

VERONA W

I've seen things being done by God. When Grandma was in hospital after her stroke, we were in church, me and my two sisters. Dad was working the Sunday. When he got home, the hospital phoned and said that Grandma had gone. Dad ran down to the car and went to the hospital. He prayed and prayed and prayed. And Grandma came round.

That has to be one of the biggest things I've seen, the biggest thing. I put it down to God, definitely. I don't think it's possible to explain. I mean, it's a miracle. She was literally dead and she came back again.

MARTIN W

I came, like most people from abroad, with a lot of bright ideas. I wanted to do this, I wanted to do that. I got into the rag trade first, then did a bit of modelling. I liked dressing up, going to parties, having a lot of high-class friends. I thought, 'There's nothing hotter than me, man. I can make it!'

After I had my family, I got into nursing. I began to see life differently. I saw suffering. I saw poverty. I saw hurt. I saw so many things, and I began to ask myself whether there was more to life than this. I began to feel there was something wrong. There was a vacuum in my life, something missing.

Then I became ill. No-one was able to say what I was suffering from, but I was going from hospital to hospital, feeling all the life in me ebb away.

One day a French lady in the next bed was telling me about her honeymoon. While she was talking, I can only describe my feeling as a yearning. Like when a pregnant woman yearns for something. Only it wasn't a mango I wanted, or some pickle. I was lying across my bed, and I said, out of the blue, 'I want Jesus.' I began to weep. The nurses thought I was going out of my mind.

As I lay on the bed, I started to hear footsteps, heavy footsteps, coming up the ward. I wasn't sleeping but I was still crying. I heard the footsteps come up the ward then stop at the foot of my bed. I felt a shadow over me, so I opened my eyes. All I saw was a sort of silhouette. I was beginning to wonder myself whether I was going mad. I began to pray. I felt such a peace and a calm.

Next day, a Pentecostal minister visited me. He said, 'You shouldn't be in hospital. There's nothing physically wrong with you. Your sickness is spiritual. The Lord wants your life to be transformed and you're fighting.'

He gave me his card and when the hospital discharged me, I phoned the number. He and his wife came round and they prayed with me. I tell you, from then my life has changed. I'd found this joyful happening in my soul, whatever it was – I wasn't quite sure – and it made me feel good.

YVONNE

W hen I met Raymond, my husband, everything just happened so fast. I could see that God was with me. I knew what I was doing. But I was really concerned that things were happening so quickly in our relationship. Then the Lord spoke to me. He said I must go on a three-day fast.

So I went on three days' fast. I got up in the morning and didn't have anything to eat or drink until night-time. I went to college and just prayed. I confessed all my sins and I prayed and I cried. Inside I was wondering. But I didn't feel nervous or hungry or anything.

On the third day the Spirit spoke to me. (You just sit there and you hear this voice speaking to you.) It was saying that this man is your husband. I said, 'Well, I think I'm doing the right thing, Lord!' We were married on 31 May 1992.

Fasting is a thing you have to do when God wants to use you, wants to speak to you. You have to clean out your vessel. You can't go dirty.

People in this community will fast quite often. Normally they fast when they have problems or they need to know what's happening in their lives, which step to take. If you're getting married, you want to know if it's the right thing. Or if you want to buy a house, you might fast about that. You ask God to guide you.

At college at the moment, I will fast and say to God, 'I want you to help me pass my exams.' It's a sacrifice. You give things up. You starve yourself. I always break a fast at night, though. Eleven o'clock is the longest I've gone through to. Somehow you get strength the more you pray.

DESREEN S

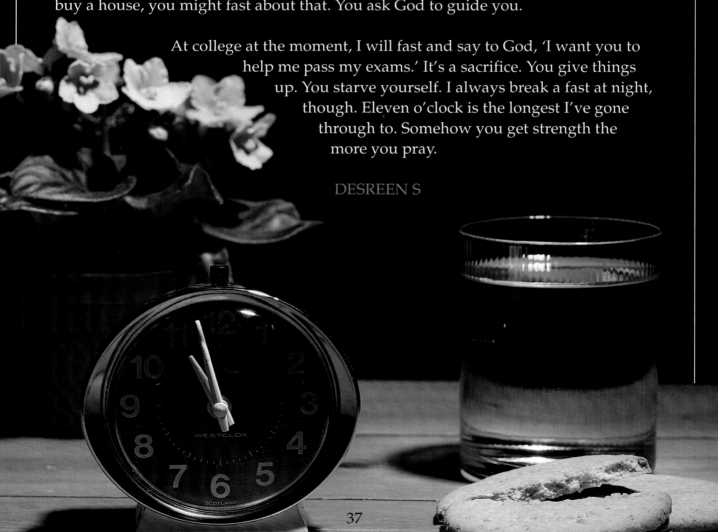

At the end of twenty years' nursing, I wanted to leave. Before I did, I thought, 'I've got to pray. God's got to help me get out of this situation.' I wanted to go into probation work and help people that way. So I prayed.

As faith would have it, my son Asa was going to school in Wimbledon. That day, driving him over, we saw one of his friends and stopped, picked him up. His mother was with him, so I offered her a lift, and we started chatting. I happened to say I wanted to go into probation. She said, 'Good. My mother's a probation officer.'

That Sunday, she arranged for me to see her mother. Her mother got me doing some voluntary work in the Probation Service. That was my stepping-stone into probation.

Eventually, I applied to do my Certificate of Qualification in Social Work. There was just one college I wanted to go to. They say you're not to lay all your eggs in one basket, but I trust God I did. And I got an interview.

The morning of that interview, I picked up an old calendar with a Bible verse printed on it. It was Psalm 37, verse 4: 'Delight yourself in the Lord and he shall grant thee the desires of thine heart.' I understood what it meant. I said, 'Lord, thank you.'

I wasn't nervous. I was so convinced I was going to pass this interview. So when the letter came two weeks later, I wasn't surprised that I'd got through. God knew my desire was to get into the Probation Service, and he kept his promise. He does, so often he does. I do believe in God's word.

JUDITH D

FACT-FINDER

Psalm 37
A psalm is a sacred song or hymn. You can find Psalm 37 in the Book of Psalms in the Bible. This is a very ancient collection of psalms still used today by both Christians and Jews.

WORDS THAT MEAN A LOT TO ME

A n important word is 'love'. My hero is Martin Luther King. There's no doubting the immense love that he had for the people around him, for the poor, for his enemies. It was fantastic.

Paul writes in Romans: 'What shall separate me from the love of God?' 'Nothing,' he says. 'Not shipwreck or famine or nakedness, nothing.' He's really inviting all the world to come against him, just to prove what he says is true! I want that to be my experience. Let everything come and I'll see what happens.

Love is the grounding for all that I do. I might not be able to preach effectively or sing effectively or anything else, but let me love God.

In fact, God has tested me on that. I was doing community work in a hostel and a person there came up to me and spat in my face. It was a test. God was telling me, 'You say you love? OK, just try this.' And I was able to rise up.

It was a good feeling. God had helped me love my enemy. God had put that love in me so that I could reach out to someone who was angry and bitter. Through me God could reach out and change that person's life.

DAVID

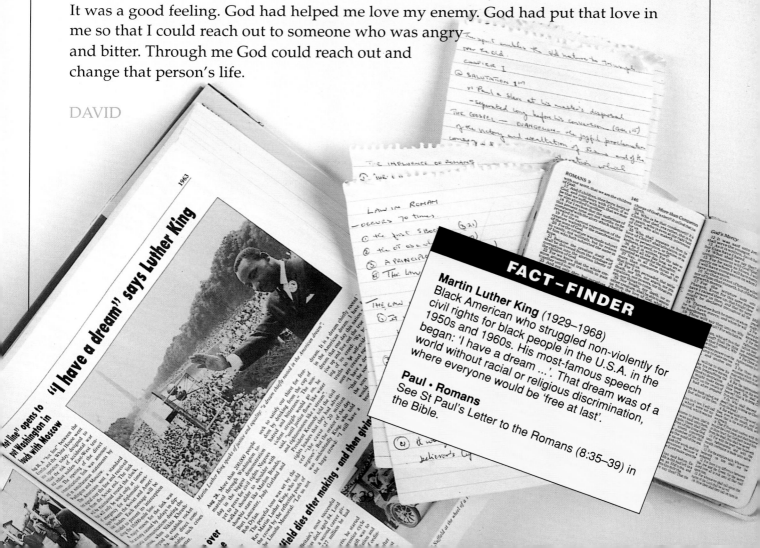

FACT-FINDER

Martin Luther King (1929–1968)
Black American who struggled non-violently for civil rights for black people in the U.S.A. in the 1950s and 1960s. His most-famous speech began: 'I have a dream ...'. That dream was of a world without racial or religious discrimination, where everyone would be 'free at last'.

Paul • Romans
See St Paul's Letter to the Romans (8:35–39) in the Bible.

I suppose the words I like most are in songs that relate to the Crucifixion. Like 'When Jesus was on the cross', 'An old woody cross', or 'On a green hill far away' – that sticks in my mind from when I was a young child.

You think of Jesus with his cross, carrying his cross to that hill at Calvary. This is the Son of God carrying his cross to a hill where he was baited by Romans and left to die in the middle of hell. That always sticks in my mind, the picture of his hands and the nails being driven in. It affects me sometimes, the amount of pain he went through.

RAYMOND S

I haven't got any favourite words as such. I like the songs. I just hum along, sing along, play along. I know my songs, but I haven't got an actual favourite.

MARTIN W

Words are important because they let you do things. Like praising God, this wonderful way of communicating with him, giving him your all. I know that he never forsakes you, and I do refer to his scriptures, where he promises to be with us.

I also like the Lord's Prayer – that really keeps me going – and 'The Lord is my shepherd'.

VERONA W

FACT-FINDER

Scriptures ...
Verona means the Bible, perhaps Romans 8:35–39.

The Lord's Prayer
Jesus gave his followers instructions on how to pray, including the words of this prayer. (See Matthew 6:9–13 in the Bible.) There are several different English translations of the Lord's Prayer.

'The Lord is my shepherd'
Well-known Christian hymn based on Psalm 23 in the Bible.

My grandmother used to say to me, 'Cast your bread on the water and days after you will find it.' It's Ecclesiastes 11, verse 1. As a child I didn't understand what she meant. Casting your bread on water? Surely it's going to rot or get waterlogged.

But as an adult I grew to understand. I was abroad, on my own in nursing, not knowing anyone, in a strange environment. People were so kind to me, and I often remember that verse. Grandmother was telling us to be kind to people because later someone might be kind back to you.

There are times now when my son complains: 'Mum, you're always running around doing things for other people.' I'm saying to him, 'Yes, I've got to do this. There's a part of me that has to. It's my nature. I enjoy doing it. And I'm not doing it for myself. It's for you. One day, someone will be kind to you.'

JUDITH D

FACT-FINDER

Ecclesiastes
The name of a book in the part of the Bible which Christians call the Old Testament.

I always turn to words in the Bible. But I must confess, I don't take up a Bible every day and religiously read. When I was growing up in my family home, I got to know a lot of the situations and experiences in the Bible, and they're in my memory.

So most of the time I draw from what's within. Because, for example, if I was down and didn't know exactly where to turn to in the Bible, how would I cope? Suppose I'm shipwrecked or the victim of some disaster and I think I'm going to die. Would I have a Bible to turn to then?

If you can hear God from within, he can minister to you. There are times when God will give me passages from the Bible and I'll dwell on them. One passage which really keeps me going is in Psalms 26, about keeping my integrity: 'I've trusted also in the Lord; therefore I shall not slide.' That's been a real source of strength for me. God has always made me feel special.

DAHLIA

When things go wrong, I say, 'The Lord is my light and my salvation. Whom shall I fear?' That's Psalms 27, verse 1. If people around me try to do things that are wrong, I say, 'Whom shall I fear?' It's God. God is able to do all things. It doesn't matter what people try to do, God's power is greater.

There's this verse from Psalms 24 as well: 'The earth is the Lord's, and the fulness thereof; the world, and they that dwell therein.'
It doesn't matter what people try to do, God still reigns.
His power is still there. We must accept it.
He's alive.

DESREEN S

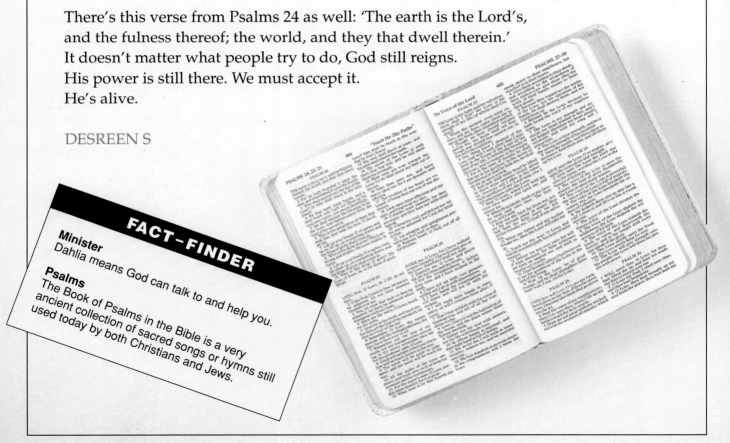

FACT-FINDER

Minister
Dahlia means God can talk to and help you.

Psalms
The Book of Psalms in the Bible is a very ancient collection of sacred songs or hymns still used today by both Christians and Jews.